The Concrete Island
Montreal Poems 1967-71

ISBN: 0-919890-05-9

Dépôt légal, Bibliothèque nationale du Québec
2e trimestre 1977.

THE CONCRETE ISLAND

Montreal Poems 1967-71

George Bowering

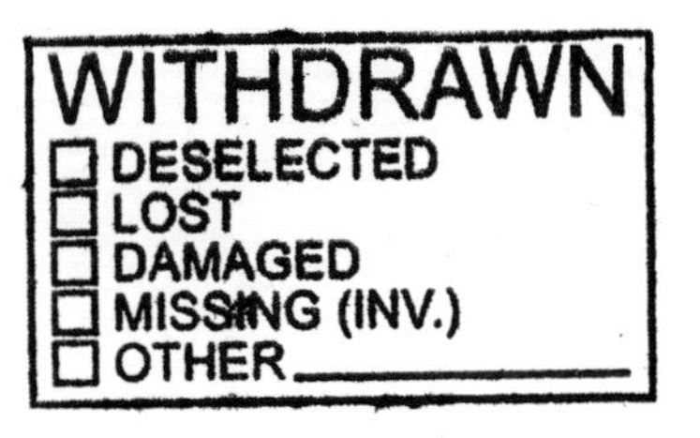

Montréal, Canada

for Artie Gold & Dwight Gardiner
found, around, there.

PREFACE

We moved to Montreal during the middle of 1967 Expo, & while we lived there we saw the bombs, the burning university, the baseball team with funny hats, the invasion by Canadian troops, & when the permanent nitrous fog moved below the twentieth floor windows of the Place Ville Marie we promised ourselves & then we left for the West Coast. I put my jeans & laced boots back on & lookt at my friends' faces again, a decade older, & now I was a Canadian at last.

My sojourn in the east took me out of place & took place out of my poetry. Since I discovered that there is no place east of Lake of the Woods, I had to look elsewhere to find poetry, should I look in books, yes, because they had books there rather than what is being written. And should I read the pages of the Daily *Unknown*, yes, because there one hears the touch of the marvelous, & so in Montreal I wrote my last lyrics, old habit, & my first books, or my first post-lyric books. I wrote *Genève* in Montreal, & most of *Autobiology*.

So here are my last lyrics, or some of them, the ones that speak of living in the city. A handful of others might be found in another book, & some of the short pieces I wrote in Montreal arent here. As I read the poems now I hear that I wasnt really there when I was writing. Simply, many of them compare the Coast to that concrete. Many of the others reflect rather than absorbing, detailing a daily life bereft of muthos. It's a true story, in other words.

I love Montreal but it is so slight, so young, so much younger than the bearded West Coast. So it's fitting, perhaps, that these desperate poems, seeking the lost assurances of a young poet's method, should take Montreal as their neighbourhood.

GB
Nov. 1975

Knocking

Near Ste Agathe
in the Laurentians

a woodpecker
knockt.

It was
hollow

.

These hillocks
they want to call

mountains, gentle
bending of the earth crust.

.

For birds
with no soaring wings

but strong feet
for verticle stance

the far sounding
beak on dead wood.

The Imperial West

I was not prepared for the crones of Westmount.
They sit side by side in Macy's drugstore
to order tea & bran muffins.

Order too

as they walk their dogs
to shit on the rain
on the grass, the lawns of Lower Westmount.

Bran muffins

will do that.

Summer Snow

My friend Tony Bellette
with the lamb upside down in his arms high
in the mountains
                    of Montenegro—

That was a year ago, my brain
is there, now
I'm here, under Mt. Royal
living poorly
                    on my big paychecks.

Tony says it is winter in the summer
does it, brings back
your young heart,
leaves you old enough to think.

White, Unseen

What do I see,
nuns?

on all the bridges over
St Lawrence river

somehow their black
is catching all the sun
light, they are dresses & still

dresses for all their habit
of names, & nomenclature.

Crossing a bridge—no roof
under the sun
meant for slow moving water

these sisters
under their smooth black garb
are white

as the air
around our sun.

The Plains of Abraham

The plains of Abraham
are smaller than my old school playground
in Lawrence, B.C.

But history
                    is a matter of accident,
who first played
at shooting & lying
face down in the grass.

Similarly
a separatist painter told me
my old schoolbook hero Dollard
was a crook.

Now Montreal's banks
fall prey to his children
every payday.

There is something about the province of Quebec
raises literary ridicule,
ruins poetry.

No Solitudes

"Why dont you write
a poem about separatists? "
now yr in Montreal, or
at least Westmount
for ever or at least
a winter.
From my balcony
the other yards, cubist
as taught this eye
by Greg Curnoe, but he
is in London, Middlesex County
Ontario, crushing bones
for art. Even the washing on the lines
cubist, the map of the prairies
as in my old jigsaw, to be fitted
all its straight lines. Look
at Saskatchewan, obeying the
narrowness of its north
due to the longitudes & not
Mercator. He was no Frenchman,
never in Prince Albert. Who
was also never
in Lawrence, B.C., where I
was & am still, but where
there were no Chinese as further north
27 miles in Penticton, where I was
born
to bring it all here
where I think
I command, in my own ambiguities
walking among French Canadian
black leather coats,

walking
that is, linear in the poems
as no separation makes feasible
as the Place Ville Marie names
Montreal, & in its sunset
turns on its lights, seen from
Mt. Royal, cubist but seen
with the same eye that sees angular
church domes, French
fried potatoes, long cubes
on the ground, fitting in.

Under the Spreading Chestnut Legs

Yes sir, an old man casually dropping his eyes
to the refuse baskets on Ste Catherine—

I said can I help you, Sir?
He said I'm looking for miscellaneous.

What could I do? I gave him some
out of my own pockets.

Time Capsule

So close
my tooth has broken yours
in a Mexican hotel
of naked women

that is
how I think of it now
surrounded by dentists
in Montreal.

Encapsulated
in our green car
over thousands after thousands
of miles, Canadian, American, Mexican
& back again

or next year in the heavy jet plane
sitting on clouds for four hours
till descending over pyramids
it brought us to that Spanish light

we were closer
to each other
than anything else
behind the cactus by the road.

& closer still
in memory
where anger in an Arizona cafe
is reduced to its stupid words.

You bite me once in a while
with your broken tooth
& that's the truth.

Revenge Against Lou the Dud

You can take all your fine namby pamby west coast poems
& shove them up your ass, he said.

Why yes, that'll be a new trip, I replied,
istracting his attention till I got him into position
& emptied my bowels all over his eastern establishment head.

City Stones (for Charles Reznikoff)

This synagogue on Sherbrooke Street
has a cornerstone from Jerusalem
laid 1957.

It is 1967 when I read
the English words written there

& think of Hebrew words
written on the stones
this year
in Jordan.

Man with Broom

Driving home alone or with Angela
I saw a sad 4:00 a.m. light
in the windows of one room
in a gradeschool by the road.

He's alone,
sweeping, looking at the floor
in front of him
maybe twelve more years of school.

Ranchero

So they all think
I'm a gunslinger come
out of the west,
say the last time I saw you
you were wearing buckskin.
Which was likely bluejeans
& canoe shoes, & hence
their reading,
my delicate poems some crazy
corner of the vaquero's rudimentary
mind, horseback, rolling cigarettes
with one hand & pages from
Jack London. Ah

my city, its edges in-
controvertible, the sea, the rocks,
the mountains allow
no spill. Hence the poems,
no spill,
            or as Davey took it,
no sprawl, from Olson, his sea
changes, the other city
on the other coast, softer
in my mind's geography, its wharves
falling into the chuck, that much
for softening, blur there
& in my mind, the cowboy.

In that way they are right,
the gun on the hip, steel
against personal flesh, a
reminder of hardness, but
expression? that way? what do they
read?

Oh Gunslinger, you
be careful; peacemaker at your thigh,
the Colt 45
can be used for good or evil.

This Time

Yes, men may walk in front of their shadows
in the city too, let me say this city
surrounded by rivers, reaching for that fact
upward, leaving the lower reaches often
in shadow.

Sombre steps are lost in traffic,
their walking sometimes not even felt.
They who carried the first cross to the top
of what they called so early a mountain,
made little impress on a continent, but the land mass
moved upward by their legs into their nerves.

That is still there, though you must go
to the sun alone now for that pace. The mornings
are best, walk in the morning, when the steams
are themselves rising, the sun dogs your heels
at first, you feel two suns, cut as they are
by late ideas of sky here.

Not the mount
alone is royal, you know given impetus you may
walk over it, to look down & away, watching
them suffer, aware of the huddle, the
obedience to captive trees,
the stairs for knees,
yes, remember the sun, it was not names
for this land, the maps
drawn on shipboard.

Leave off question of community, imagined
hereditary, for its building too was of shadows
of men & their makings, a shadow on sons
& grandsons, while you, the great
grandsons, may walk in front of your shadows
yet on this earth packt upward.

The Rites of Passage, Book of the Real

How I survived that
& am drawn back to it
can be pictured
as early morning the clam sky
behind slightly waving black
fir tips, the dampness
calling for hot coffee, that liquid
inside, learned from fathers,
& flat watery porridge
with canned milk
to eat with hot spoon leaning
on slash pile, boots not warm yet.

I am away from that now
wearing wine coloured French corduroy slacks
in Montreal snow, but Dorn,
Ed Dorn has it, his book made
as my father made his first tent,
with skill brought from
his secret experience.

Classic Poetry & Its Laws

Des poètes
montréalais
liront leurs
oeuvres

etcetera.

I dont know what I expected.
Naked girls with guitars over their crotches maybe.
French Canadian homosexuals jerking each other off
to the beat of a native alexandrine.
Muffins thrown in fury & croissants hurled back.
Microphones lost up the asses of Westmount elders.

We got a muddy floor, dry mouths, private police
chasing the artists from the door.

au nouveau
'Classic Bookshop'
1434 Ste-Catherine ouest

where the middle was the worst
& the ending was the best.

It's There, You Cant Deny It

The muddy snow melting
along the east side of Grosvenor Ave here

brings old dog turds to light.
They have begun to separate

into their component parts—
sixty percent grain, forty percent meat byproducts.

It's there, you cant deny it,
you cant flush it away, the ground covered

with shit. It makes you think:
at an average of a pound per day per head

New York has to hide twelve million
pounds of human shit a day

or 4.38 billion pounds a year.
The queen of England poops

three times her weight in turds a year.
In a normal lifetime she'll pile up

fourteen tons of majestic brown crap.
Ah, what do we think of ourselves

poet or queen
or the dogs in between.

Where I Am

This St Lawrence spring at last
& great day may enter as I walk
from 439 Grosvenor Ave to the 24 bus.

But the river is no more
than a line of received data
in the mind, this is no island
save wherein we have been so told.

It is in the morning paper on the bus
a seaway, an economic determinant,
highway to the Great Lakes in
another country's middle west.

Well, I have been there, & there,
I am in my body, as it contains
its own water, its own ways, I
have found place within place.

Steak & Gravy

After two days with no meat
& few vegetables we have here
        pounded minute steak with thick onion gravy
        small green peas with onion gravy
        home-fried potatoes & carrots
        green salad with oil & vinegar
        thick coffee in the pot.

Yes, it is because of the two of us
& ten dollars from a friend
a lot of oldtime slippery belly love
& a touch of spring air thru the dining room window.

School Girl Crush

Once every two weeks I see her,
the teenage girl with her fat baby lips
walking in her navy blue school skirt up Grosvenor St.

& I see chains around her pink legs,
a whip in my hand, I bring it down gently
on the backs of her thighs.

What am I saying? Is this me, or have I
read too many Brandon House novels? I've never
stubbed my cigar on a girl's breasts.

But I see her walking up the street thinking
of neat radio songs or matriculation, not dreaming
the pleasures of the velvet lash

& I want to awaken her, see the tears come
to her eyes, the convulsions of her downy belly,
whip hand Geordie, Sagittarius, the golden teacher.

Three Days on the River Island

An Englishman from New Brunswick,
an Englishman from Upper Canada,
a black haired madonna from upstate New York,
& I, long hair comic strip extra from the west

went into the lower town at Quebec
to buy a frisbee, I
make my patriotic saucer trip to Canadian history
throwing bright yellow plastic
into the wind of 18th century Ile d'Orleans.

> Where one graveyard bears names
> of three families, men in this century
> 85 years old on their stoops
> never been to the mainland, the city
> ten miles away.

My friends & I
consume products of Rheims & Boston
in our short days, never speaking the language
save to curse the TV Canadienne
showing us the gray war tanks of Prague.

Still, it splits the St Lawrence
waters of detritus & shipping on its way
like us, outward.

(Aug 1968)

Beardsley

I took the sum from the bank
& walkt along Ste Catherine
toward the football ticket store

but not past the book store
with a sale on; I bought
a book of Beardsley drawings.

Football ticket: $4.00.
Book of drawings: $3.98.

I could have gone back to the bank
for more, but my mind
doesnt work that way.

I can sit in the front room tonight
looking at the pictures,
hoping like hell that it rains.

Montreal Poets, 1968

The sad poets of Montreal
never see a snake, that cold flesh
in brown grass of say
the south Okanagan.

The lonely Montreal poets
stand without community at social
functions eyeing one another
like a younger brother.

Coming back to Montreal, I
have bought earphones for my music
so I cant hear a knock on the door
listening as I do to stereo separation
& the blood in my temples.

Once a month I see a Montreal poet
anxiously dodging taxis downtown,
expensive manuscripts almost falling,
almost, but not falling
among the feet on Sherbrooke Street.

The Other Poet's

The other poet's wife
on the black couch

has orange flowered pants
under her dress.

I look at the bent
skin there, as at

a friend. The familiar
is come at by

our own entering
stages of life. Being

poet, getting married.

Silver & Gold, The Trees

So once again they're selling
fir trees in the garage lots,
those nature-lovers, watching nature
seep out on the greasy snow
among their own feet, forgetting
what was told them.

Learn not the way of the heathen,
& be not dismayed at the signs of heaven;
for the heathen are dismayed at them.

For the customs of the people are vain:
for one cutteth a tree out of the forest,
the work of the hands of the workman,
with the ax.

They deck it with silver & with gold;
they fasten it with nails & with hammers,
that it move not.
& later they lie
in back lanes on snow on the ground
full of germs, but the garages sell
tree-shaped deodorizers, green as green
& the trees turn brown as the ground
rises to meet them in our forgetfulness.

How To Be

How to be hip in Montreal
with a French Canadian dwarf

washing our second story windows,
a four-pound dog on my lap

shivering, his head
under my armpit. I believe in

the church domes
named after the saints,

this makes a city. But today
I saw a delivery boy

carrying a carton of Coke
into the offices of Molson's

within view of Our Lady of
Bonsecours. The windows

in that part of town, they're
so filthy you cant see thru them.

Daniel Johnson Lying In State

Along the deathwatch
crowds in front of
the court house

a perfect row of police
motorcycles, silver
gray Harley
Davidsons, slant

sun off their
front fenders.

& a block away
the dead Buicks piled
upside down, twenty

feet high. They have
men in soiled coveralls
for attendants.

Oct1/68

Aloha

I'm sitting on the 24 bus
beside a lovely
Chinese girl who's reading
Interracial Marriage in Hawaii–

& thinking
Should I ask her–
naw, I just got out of
my own white bed

& this vehicle's taking me
eastward, into Montreal.

In The Elevator

In the elevator
everyone is resentful
of everyone
else's stop.

As if,
dreaming, we
could choose
our various fates.

Silent door
slowly opening sideways
with glimpses of floors
not ours, not ours.

Everyone in the box
knows where
he's going,

he only looks
at the others
when the elevator stops
between floors.

Hands & Nets

Ah, that nation *is* pacific,
I mean here
where the swells are
this eastern clime
made a political
item.

The flounder has eyes to see
all ways
lying on his
acquired belly
at the bottom. He is

a symbol I state
having seen him here
in a glass case
a study.

At Kitsilano Beach nightfall
finds men casting private nets
for smelt
for the family
that very night.
It is not a case of
dispute,

those contracts, tariffs, cross-
family accounts
but pleasure
& comfort
a matter of timing

tide & appetite shared.

Riding the 24 Bus East

Strange lone man gets on:
is he disguised as
lonely westerner of Revelstoke
as I know him?

He's wearing no Montreal winter duds
but undershirt, shirt, pullover sweater
& finally old highschool basketball jacket.
His hair is red, scar on his cheek—
some of you know what I mean,
he probably smokes roll yr owns
with his hand cupt to the hard air
on the Rogers Pass.

The grace-
ful bare trees on Westmount Park
covered with ice, that not silver
but angelic or ghostly grey
filtered & nearly destroyed light
of midmorning winter.

An icy branch scrapes the top of the bus.

& at the corner of St Matthew
there's one of those Montreal girls
with long thin legs
crost, the ice in the air
cold up them, her little blue clam
under the tiny skirt
nothing like the magazine pictures.

So I've been there
& back, leaning on my breath
against the window.

Driving Upper Westmount

But at night the icy hanging trees
are dript silverfoil
the streetlamps glow thru.

This is the last night of November
night before my birthday
& four years after his death.

So they are trees, yes, naked
with the water frozen outside,
the thin limbs asleep

outside these old successful
stone houses against whose walls
the winters live & die.

(writ stan's house)

Getting Off the 24 Bus

The old
men & women

pull twice
on the bell cord

accustomed to
asking for

questions to
be repeated.

Derelicts in the Metro Station

He walks in-
tently
to the
waste basket

making it
look like his
job.

Mandatory Spring Poem

Under a murky skylight
under cloudy St Lawrence sky
spring came today at 2:08 pm

while I read a poem
to lovely eyes of crocus
art students, long hair pusht back with painty fingers

& later across the street
it fell into whiskey glasses where
nervous teachers with hearts aching for summer

retold stories of cursing
at their secretaries about posters,
index cards, ballpoint pens, these things lovely too

as the students, as the teachers,
I may speak to them both, it is the equinox,
& we all turn to warm the other side.

Late Spring, New Week

How lovely, it is so cold
this morning, I gladly shiver

in my thin jacket, the cold air
entering my forehead

to pierce the headache there.

In the Heart of Jewish Montreal (for Curnoe etc)

At the central YMCA cafeteria
all the men in ironed suits
order roast beef & boiled potatoes

& I've just moved here
from Upper Canada. I take out
my I.B. Singer book, what else?

Flesh Cushion

Just when the leaves
have made rounded forms
of this backyard's bones

these two kids
try to set fire
to that wetness.

        I've been
watching them from my balcony
knowing they really couldnt
keep it going

                    & knowing
this is the first time
I've stood idle & staring
since last November.

        Spring works
its ways upon us, in its ways
more than one.

Otherwise Nobody Would Ever Have Remembered Joe

I've been out from two this afternoon
till two this morning
& she hasnt askt me where I been,
sitting in there reading
her seventeenth century rhetoric.

Would you believe it, sweetie? I went
six hours without a smoke
sitting in Mary Brown's front room
watching a twenty inning game
& the Red Sox won on a home run by Joe Lahoud
just when she came home.

But if I told her that if
she wanted to ask if
things hadnt been the way they
were at two this afternoon

I'd say John Donne would have
liked that.
& she would say
no he wouldnt.

First New England Jag

If I were a plant
this high branch shadow
along the Vermont road
would be my sunshine.

Here where for the first time
in a year I have to
steer the car, I'm alone
& those two memories

are second to sitting
in front of an absent friend's
shack, watching his creek
send drink past him.

I'm drunk with that,
off the concrete island, back
home nearly, in the middle
of this gentle British
Columbia.

(St. Johnsbury)

A DP in Time

Who says
standing four steps off the bag
at second for the York Street Tigers

I'm not on the lip
of Eternity, is that
the name of the place?

Because your timing
means seeing the hip-swing
out of time's basepath
making the double play

& it only takes a poet
good on the pivot
two seconds to become
one of the game's immortals.

Okay, Layton Etc., Women Like Poems

I want to run around
fucking all of them
the most beauteous or the one with
round jaunty bum, the other
with big lips, I'll enter
what way I can.

Whereas my friend might say
stay with one, with her, learn
all she can show you, drain
all her juices
that will return again.

Yes but, yes
but there she goes, & there
she goes, twitching that thing
thru a doorway, &

there I go, pen in hand
or you name it, I mean it's like . . .

or rather: remember, I also
move my home every year or two.
All the time I'm living here
there are cities going on
over there, & there

& they're filled with beauteous women
& poems, &
I'll take her with me, or
I'll let her take me, too.

Safe in Westmount

The news papers say the Concrete Island
is on fire,
last night the police
went on strike & the city was given over
to "bands of vandals"—

The American tourist at the Queen Elizabeth hotel said
I can understand this happening in Watts, but not
in the middle of downtown.

When the Romans
took over the far parts
of the world

they spoke
the local language
for greater control.

I lay in my bed by the window
in Westmount, counting
the explosions. One two three—

I Take

I take my underwear off at night
& stand naked for a given time.
The prime minister takes his underwear off
& stands naked for a given time.
What but time is given
to the lonely keypunch operator girl
taking off her underwear & standing
in front of her mirror before she goes
to her single bed midnight some
snow-surrounded corner of the city
encircled by the frozen river?
What am I giving by the tired wrist
crampt to write these words? What is time
to give, that is steadily dropt away,
48 minutes of a basketball game gone
into fading familiar history re-enacted
for money next year's season? While
all the time it fades away time-out or not.
What about the dream of standing naked
in collapst time an hour or lifetime
in fifteen seconds of the prime minister's
prime time? Why dont we keep the underwear on
& stare down
concentrating on your naked feet
stepping up & down, bony toes
marking where you stand,
where you are standing,
keeping time,
trying to keep the time.

Montreal, Oct 1970

The soldiers standing all day
in front of rich houses,
they're all wearing American helmets now.

So what? We live here. They have just
brought them outdoors. They carry
automatic rifles & peer thru big eyeglasses.

It is the latest language from Ottawa
recruiting drive, dull us a little
as we walk past a gun muzzle without flinching.

Last night on Crescent St. the feathered kids
still stand there among the spots
of shit from their fancy lank dogs.

The army visits from the farm for awhile,
how you going to keep them at our expense,
who cares where they stand, who knows
a soldier's name?

Very well then we are two nations,
one inside one out, is it a jeweled escapement,
is it a door, the imported automatic rifle?

Bus Step

I take
delight in giving
the exact fare.

Coming to Montreal From Vancouver

The difference
here
is the drama
the concrete island
made for it,
history & drama, no
geology to mess it up,
no sea to swallow it.

So the magazines, the public
press
to get at it, explain
the French fact,
the countryside so often ugly
but the city, they say,
the character
& the characters, the violence, they say,
the incident,
a play usually
without yr own words,
that play
unnecessary,
the daily news so much
there.

There, finally, is why the government
said restrict the war measures act
to the Quebec problem,
how
could you do otherwise? how
avoid the roar of the crowd, the captive
audience when they come on stage, all
of them.

Our coast
is lyric, the eyes
look constantly outward,
there is
nowhere else, & inward, the cones
intersecting
one by one, no manager

yet (tho they try, they filter into
our land, we have workt so hard to say
our)
boundaries are yet to be
defined & that is the work, a lonely
art,
no theatre & no stars to solo
above the composition.

Acknowledgements

Some of these lyrics appeared first in the following:
Anthology (CBC); **The Ant's Forefoot**; **The Capilano Review**; **Fifteen Winds** (Ryerson, 1969); **The Fifth Estate**; **The Georgia Straight**; **Hanging Loose**; **Hyphid**; **Iron**; **Manroot**; **The McGill Daily** Supplement; **The Montrealer**; **Montreal Poems**; **The Mysterious East**; **The Nation**; **Noose**; **Only Humans With Songs To Sing**; **Poetry Australia**; **Quarry**; **Sunday Supplement** (CBC); TV Sir George.

Other books by George Bowering

Genève, 1970
Autobiology, 1971
Curious, 1973
In the Flesh, 1973
Flycatcher, 1974
At War With the U.S., 1975
Allophanes, 1976

Cover design: Rick Fischer
Published with assistance from the Canada Council.

Printed & published in an edition of 500
March 1977 by Véhicule Press, P.O.Box 125,
Station 'G', Montreal, Canada.